AF673868

BITTERSWEET

John Grey

ISBN: 978-93-6354-580-9

First Edition: 2025
Rs. 200/-

Cyberwit.net
HIG 45 Kaushambi Kunj, Kalindipuram
Allahabad - 211011 (U.P.) India
http://www.cyberwit.net
Tel: +(91) 9415091004
E-mail: info@cyberwit.net

Printed at Repro India Limited.

Contents

Bittersweet

Sad cafes,
dying campfire,
and the echo
of a marble hallway –
those are my gods.

And they are my perspectives.

Where I drink alone,
where I sleep alone,
where I live alone.

The view from here
is cold and tired,
lacks warmth
and other voices.

Yet I don't complain.

Not now.
Not when I have a poem to please.

An Intuit Boy

In the boy's small bedroom,
a polar bear repeats itself
across the wallpaper.

The many splashing seals
have no fear
of the giant white predator.
Nor does the slinking
Arctic fox.

A row of salmon fly
smoother than
the watchful owls.

And the whiskers
of the walruses
are ticklish to the eye.

His favorite are the malamutes,
pack after pack
eager to be off and running,

He drifts off to sleep
grabbing hold of their reins.

Tonight, they bring him home.
Someday, they'll whisk him out of here.

Dead Man?

Terrified sometimes
of how, when
I bend down to
peer into the cool spring
mountain stream,
that a face could be looking up at me.

A man fades out of his own photographs.
Another goes silent in the grave.
A third was just a target anyhow,
from without, from within.
I knew them.
I watched their disintegration
from up close.

But what if it's a stranger?
An army vet
with three missions
trapped inside his brain cells.
A woman battered to death
by the man she married?
A child who ventured
too close to the edge?

I've fished in these waters.
I've even swum.
But those were good days
and I've had bad ones.
And the worst of all

would roll out of these mountains,
ride the current
right when I'm thinking
today is going to be a great day.

What if the body
sheds a limb,
bursts an eye,
thumps against my dangling fingers?
Terrified sometimes
that I've lived this long
without this one thing happening.
Look up there.
A shape – can't quite make it out –
it's rolling this way.
If it's something,
it's on its way downstream.
If it's someone,
it's headed straight for me.

Tropical Escape

From a cramped motel room,
I launch myself into bright seaside air.

In shorts, tee-shirt and sandals,
I am Summer Man, Shoreline Man.

The person you thought you knew –
the guy in the coffee-house,

all sweatered-up for the winter,
head face down in a book,

is no more. At least, he's been set aside,
placed in mothballs, while his inner moth

is drawn to the broad, shameless light.
I cross the busy coast road,

take the wooden bridge over sea-grass dunes,
step onto sand that gives way as much

as it supports, half-run that giddy way
I did as a child with knees bent, arms flapping,

as the waves and I meet half-way up the beach,
and bare toes turn magically into foam.

This poem is being written by the one
you thought you knew – coffee house guy,

head face down in a notebook while
his pen and memory scribble lines.

It is all about primal pleasure.
Yet only Winter Man can describe it.

Suburbia, On Any Given Day

Steve is comforted by the fact that humans are top of the food chain.
His sister Keri's greatest wish is for some cute guy
to stand beneath her window and sing Harry Styles songs to her.
If it's the actual Harry Styles, so much the better.
To their mother, Harriet, everything is a matter of life and death.
Her husband, Frank says you must make trouble's strength work against it.
Harriet long ago threw up her hands at the ever-changing world of fashion.
Steve's best friend, Kurt would like nothing more than an inner being.
Keri's paranoid about all the minute creatures crawling on her skin.
Frank was the last person in his graduating class to own a laptop.
Keri's best friend, Hannah can't swim but can often be found posing,
at the town pool, at the very end of the diving board.
Steve considers his parents to be small-minded.
Kurt so much wanted a drum kit for his birthday
but his divorced mom bought him a rifle instead.
Frank has an abnormal fear of being sued for slander.
Hannah's dad, Roy is always saying how there's more than one way
to skin a cat.
He can only name one.
Steve longs for powers beyond those of mortal men.
When Kurt grows up, he wants to be a slumlord.
Keri's on-and-off boyfriend, Derrick collects critters in jars.
Harriet considers rap artists the worst of humanity.
In her teenage years, she worshiped Guns 'n' Roses.
Steve has yet to find any use for his self-choreographed victory dance.
When Keri is ten years older, she plans to take stock of her life.
Roy has sold fewer used cars this year than all three of his co-workers.
Hannah's often found on her front doorstep, rehearsing how to say
goodbye to a guy.

Kurt's experiences with bullies have been fearful and demeaning
but, as yet, none have ended in bloodshed.
Harriet possesses nothing that will increase in value in the coming years.
Having lived all his life in the suburbs, Frank has never been
in a position where he had to find a needle in a haystack.
When Roy writes out a check for his mortgage payment,
he deliberately doesn't cross the t's or dot the i's.
Steve, recently introduced to tacos, is yet to make up his mind
as to whether he likes them or not.
Frank, always a team player, once dreamed of being
the third guy from the left in a firing squad.
Hannah is comforted by the fact that no terrorist attacks
have ever been carried out in a suburban setting.
Roy is the only one at the lot who still reads the newspaper funny pages.
Steve is a major reason behind Frank's vasectomy.
Derrick often says, if he had it all to do over again, he wouldn't
change a thing.
The frog (name unknown) in his biggest, smelliest jar, is of a different
mindset.
Explaining My Heart To You
My heart is a tossed salad - I hope you like greens.
My heart is a rusty, abandoned railcar -
the graffiti says it all.
My heart is a field of wheat - tossed about
with just the merest breath of wind.
My heart is the dying embers of a fire -
some glow, a little warmth,
but not enough to stave off real bitterness.
My heart is like a child who will eat
nothing but what's bad for him -
please, keep on with the spoon-feeding.
My heart could play drums in a jazz combo -
its beat is more syncopated than steady.

My heart is an annoying yapping dog -
anything for attention and yes, it chews the rug.
My heart is a gasbag - poem after shameless poem.
My heart is a dead ringer for a painting of Jesus
by artists who had no clue what the man looked like.
So stand and stare like you're really appreciating
that big, sloppy organ.
My heart is the guy who prefers 'Godfather III'
to the first two - it impresses those who haven't
seen any of the trio.
My heart is generous to a fault - so why don't
the faults ever thank it?

In A World That Only Involves Ducks

Lake ice is breaking up
and the ducks find room
for webbed feet to breathe.
A male pintail's wheezy "prip prip"
is answered by a female's quack.
A canvasback flutters white feathers
behind a proud brown head.
A wood duck flashes its red eye
as it dabbles in the thawing waters.

Most ducks form swimming flocks.
But a few pair off, slip away
like covert lovers
into the privacy of the shoreline reeds.
New life beckons.
Old life heeds the call.

Indian Summer

The sun of Indian summer
moves slowly across boundaries
that seasons have created to divide us,
crimson spotlights blazing through
the mists of imaginary borders,
the filter of trees,
redrawing the map of tribes and species,
gilding the pond, the grass-tips,
rescuing park benches
from emptiness's chill.

Now twilight sparkles
the half-molted forest,
oaks and elms
that can't believe their luck.

Even the moon
rises vast and orange,
as if it holds the warm day
for safekeeping.

No longer the last refuge
of November light,
it glows with all the small prayers
that put it there.

To The Fox

The fox is wild and yet
he comes up closer to the house
than any neighbor.

His fur is russet gray,
his domain the haze of twilight.

I see him from the porch,
sniffing at the garden,
swishing his bushy tail back and forth
like a friendly dog.

But then he looks up at me,
a stare fit both for friend or foe,
while his open mouth reveals
a row of sharp teeth,
a smile that inhales a snarl
then blows it out again.

He then slips through a hole in the back fence,
one too small for my body.

Slowly he retreats to the woods beyond.
Not in fear, merely incompatibility.

The Car Alarm

I walk by a parked car
and the alarm goes off,
startles me like a hand
touching my shoulder
in the dark.

Maybe it was my after-shave
that set the thing whooping
or just my aura
or my thoughts.

I'm the only one around here
so I feel responsible,
guilty even.

Surely there's someone,
even now,
up in their third-floor apartment,
staring down at me
as if I'm the most disreputable
man on the planet.

Could be they're already calling the cops.

I can imagine the sirens and the shouts –
"He did it! He did it!"

Then I hear a beep,
the cars' lights flash,
and the alarm stops dead.

Either some guy pressed his remote
or the jury returned its verdict.

The Guy At The Open Mike

He wore frayed blue overalls.
His close-cropped hair
would have passed muster
in army boot camp.

He sat stone-faced
at a coffee-house table,
a few scraps of paper
spread before him,
sipping on coffee
as black as what
most everyone else was wearing
in that basement dive.

It was an open poetry reading,
the usual stream of monotone-voiced sufferers
of every emotional malady
that ever spread its sensory viruses
through the written word.

Someone asked if he wanted to read
but he shook his head.
"My stuff's just shit," he sighed.

Next up was a blood-clot on two legs
whining about Christopher Columbus
followed by a girl
with face so pale and white
you could have mistaken her
for a page intentionally left blank.

He said he worked second shift
in a factory,
jotted things down from time to time
about stuff he knew
like work and riding his motor bike.
"Besides," he added,
"my voice is raspy
and people find the way I talk
tough to understand."

Open mike went on
without him
but sorely in need of him.
The Family Wanderer

The wanderer
suddenly
finds himself
walking backwards
through the front gate
of the family home,
up the path,
the three steps to the door,
where many hands await
ready to push him
firmly back in
the opposite direction.

If he can
get by them
it's as if he
never left.

For Worse

I plan to be generous with just about everything
Love is only the beginning.
There are also my books to be considered,
my collection of old vinyl,
my habits of course,
my taste in food and television
and, let's not forget,
my infatuation with ancient
Fred Astaire and Ginger Rogers movies.
When I said "I do"
under the nose of the priest,
in front of that conglomeration
of friends and family,
I made a commitment to not hold back
one New England Patriots cap,
any Playboy magazines,
an addiction to Coca Cola
and an appreciation for all things Disney.
The honeymoon is over
and up from the cellar,
like the Beast from 20,000 Fathoms,
comes my collection of souvenirs
from my trip to Paris,
while down from the attic,
like heavy smelly snowflakes,
float the sneakers I will never wear again
but haven't the heart to throw away.
I'm sorry sweetheart.

This is your reward
for agreeing to marry me.
Yes, you get the man before you now.
But I'm just how these things start.

In Ghoul World

If it could, the entire planet would stop
for every road accident.
The Indian mystic, Chinese farmer,
and the Portuguese fishermen
would gladly halt what they were doing
to witness a three-car pileup on 95.
They could join the South African minister,
the French chef and the Irish politician,
in saying out loud, "I hope nobody's seriously hurt."
And then there's the monk from Myanmar,
the Hungarian horse trainer and
the Australian jackeroo
who'd be giving thanks that they're not the ones
being dragged from that crumpled-up metal.
Instead, it's all locals that slow down
for a view of what's happening,
combine a brief prayer with ghoulish curiosity.
They feel twice lucky.
Lucky that they're not involved.
Lucky that somebody was.

The Lessons In Arguing

An argument drags up
other, older arguments -
fighting knows the past
better than memory.
We blow off on tangents.
We find the connection
between this hurt
and its long dormant grandfather.
We're overwhelmed
like children with too many toys at Christmas.
Only we break our toys.
We'd even break Christmas if we could.

An argument needs to be this way.
It can't be centered.
It must never be linear.
A rational argument on either side
and there'd be no hope for us.
Irrational is the only hope.
A viewpoint must, for the good of all,
eventually sound crazy to the person saying it.

So I can't play cards with the guys
because the iron's cord is frayed.
Your mother won't visit with us
as long as there's a nasty noise
in the Volvo's engine.

You're calm.
I'm feeling better now.
We kiss and make up.
I'd like to see logic try.

The Sonnet Of The Forest

My estimation of surrounding trees
Changes in context with advancing hours,
From the hopeful, light-tinged morning bowers
To vibrant forest greening by degrees
Into such lush and languid reveries
Of breeze-blown bough and abundant flowers
To twilight's radiant gold-tipped towers,
Thick tapestries of verdant majesties.

But come the nighttime, come pervading gloom,
The shadow woodland is a disquiet lair,
A moonless crypt, an arboreal tomb,
A shapeless, haunting, dungeon of despair.
Not buoyant life but doleful dreaded doom
Of nothing to see and yet surely there.

To A Cop Found Hanging

When the fire spoke,
it was in the language of a crackling toy train,
not a small boy. Yes, his toy train crackled.
The caboose exploded,
bits of metal flying everywhere.
I held a hot sliver in my hand when it occurred to me.
I don't speak burning metal.
The ashes couldn't tell me anything but that's ashes all over.

Couldn't find the corpse, but by the sound of
the blood's conversation, I could tell that
the witnesses were lying to me - it wasn't some tart
but delicate, demure, pursed lips, a nose, a freckle -
a young woman surely - DNA lifted its skirts
to reveal a long, lithe brown leg.
But despite the bludgeoning he gave her, she didn't know
the guy. Then she dried into a stain and said no more.

Guys had to dig and dig just to get
a word out of those basement bones.
Mostly, it was me putting words into their mouths -
we take the blame, we were foolish, we thought he was a kind man -
I tap-tapped on the skull for good measure. No tap-tap back.
Skulls are useless with Morse code.

My problem is I figure victims want nothing more
than to set their stories straight.
But rope scars look up at me with such a puzzled look.
A hanging? This neck? That ceiling beam? You're joking, right?

I've placed a severed human finger to my ear just like a shell -
nothing - likewise, the dismembered leg and the liver
that came gift-wrapped.
Talk to a body encased inside a cement block -
you may as well be talking to a cement block.

Friends tell me maybe I should hang out with the living for a while.
I can see through them. They just want to know who did this to me.

Dear Friend

Yes,
I miss you,
I love you.

But the funeral was a disaster.
Everyone tried to put you into words.
The ceremony was an off-kilter tribute
to how much they failed.

Not one laugh
and yet the speakers assured us all
that they knew you.
So where were the pratfalls?
Where were the giddy highs
overwhelming the bruises?

Instead we were force-fed
a thousand and one banalities,
scenes set, memories,
that could have been of any one.

I longed to point out
who exactly it was up there
in his best suit, arms folded,
staring up at the ceiling
from the soft depths of his coffin.

A man has died, I wanted to say.
Let us not be what killed him.

My Collection

I know what's supposed to happen to all these cans.
Once I'm done drinking out of them
they go into the recyclable bin
which sits out on the sidewalk overnight Tuesday
so the truck can pick them up
and take them to the reclaimable center.

But I'm not the man I was.
I'm in a mood these days to preserve
rather than just let things go.
Maybe my ex has something to do with that.
Hold onto what you got was her credo.
Well I got a lot of these cans.

So maybe I'll store them in the cellar.
Or why not in the bedroom.
They'll be right at home there
with all that emptiness.

Some guys collect stamps,
others, old 78's.
Me, I figure I'll start accumulating
empty beer cans.
One thing about signs of weakness,
there's strength in numbers.

The Beauty Begins Here

It's a multicolored Autumn forest,
and I understand implicitly
that the trees are giving their all,
the life of their leaves mostly,
just to impress me.

But I'm also fully aware,
that the forest floor
is a graveyard,
though the fallen leaves cackle underfoot,
"I am not dead."

Not a graveyard really.
More of the scene of a sacrifice,
a season's worth of greenery
beginning its mulching path
toward future Springs.

It's an insight into beauty's true nature.
Fragility with strength.
Penance and reparation.
Beautiful.
Nature.

A Suburban News Update

Will has never been the type to be bound by petty conventions.
He's out of detox and back roaming the strip clubs.
His girlfriend, Sarah has stood by him,
despite his being the one she had to settle for
after Scott announced his engagement to Kami.
Will's father Roy has never felt deprived for having no imagination.
Roy's wife Cilla, helps out in the community but is seldom
thanked.
Sarah's mother Kate bursts into tears when she drives by
a boarded-up K-Mart store.
Kate's husband, Sam says to everyone he meets,
"You've got to have money if you want to make money."
Sarah's little brother, Paul wants to be on the lam when he grows up.
Will's brother Joey gets upset when Roy won't show him the
Mason handshake.
Ever since he was a child, Will has had this plastic bag phobia.
If only his mother had never warned him, "A plastic bag is not a toy."
Paul is proud of all the shit he's pulled.
Scott once beat up a kid within an inch of his life.
Kami's claim to fame is that her name starts with a K.
Will's grandfather, Big Will, is shorter and weighs less than his
grandson.
Joey's been researching job opportunities in the field of football
mascots.
Roy tells him that if law school doesn't work out there's always
pizza delivery.
Cilla's horoscope says this is a good week for a workplace
romance
but she sells real estate and her only co-worker is sixty year old Vivian.

Kate is involved in something called "Puppies For Portly People."
Sam says, to no one in particular, "That's not body odor, it's man perfume."
Will first earned his parent's ire when it became obvious
he would not remain a chubby little baby forever.
For all of his predilection for arson, Paul has yet to burn down anything significant.
Kami's friends want to slap her face when she talks about her growth as a person.
Roy has never found a use for staring up at the night sky.
Joey is adamant that nothing can ever make learning fun.
Sarah is not a cat person but she wouldn't say no to looking like Cat Woman.
Will wasn't fired from his part-time job. He quit.
Sam once came close to being an innocent bystander.
Roy has been fed up with politics from the age of eleven.
Cilla's childhood dream was to someday be a trendsetter.
Paul can't come out to play. He just killed the dog.
Sam knows just enough about his boss's personal affairs
to never be at risk of being replaced by a machine.
Will just learned he was conceived in the backseat of a Buick.
Twenty years to the day it may be,
but Cilla remains unimpressed by the best sex she ever had.
Kate is jealous because her so-called friend Anita has a personal trainer.
And, worst of all, Anita isn't actually training for anything.
If You Wish To Know My Current Location

I live on the tire
swinging out over the lake,
with my hands around the tadpole jar,
completely fascinated by
a scoopful of mud
and quivering eye-lash things.

That's me in the old camper,
flopped on the mattress,
behind the door that doesn't quite close.

I'm on all the places on the map
where there are woods, an amusement park,
or a pinball arcade.

Or by some fishing hole
unknown to Rand McNally
where brook trout donate
their own life's journey
to the worm I dangle underwater.

I spend my time
in the saddle of a John Deere,
going "brm brm brm"
as if the monster was moving.

Look for my first taste of chocolate
or raisin bread
or my soft hands pressed painfully
on the steel strings of a guitar.
I'll be there.

Such a warm comforting, endearing, place.
I'm the farthest thing from death
I can imagine.

The Poem Of The Hunters

It's October
and the woods are riddled with hunters.
Mostly guys, a few women,
they're adorned in orange,
toting shotguns,
and ready to kill the first creature
bigger than a chipmunk
that wanders into their rifle sights.

The forest is mostly this empty chamber
but, come fall,
every slot is filled with death.
My advice is to not be a deer
or a bear or duck
when the likes of you are in season.
But nature doesn't listen to me.
The song of autumn
is an array of blasting weaponry
Hunters high-five as
the body count ratchets up.

I find that I can't get inside
the proud stag's mind.
What he feels, all he fears,
are unknown to me.
But the hunter is a mystery to me also.
Never in my life
have I felt the urge
to take up a gun and shoot something.

So hunting's this collision course
between a prey I have no concept of
and a predator whose sensibilities
have nothing in common with mine.

I can only make it cruel, a waste.
I could never get by on understanding.

Walking In The Winter Forest

Without their leaves,
maples are not maples.
They're just bare trees
with wind-shaken shadows.
And where are the oaks?
Not these dead men surely –
buried upright but
bare-boned corpses every one.

My presence teases them
with movement, touch,
and mist-tinged breathing.
Sure, their roots go deep.
But I'm the one on a
brisk and healthy morning walk.
They do no more than
nibble on the soil beneath
for paltry winter sustenance.

For a good three miles,
my footsteps crunch
the brown-leaf trails,
scatter the remaining birds
and nervous squirrels,
the dregs of spring and
summer's bountiful wildlife.

And yet, a month or two
from now, resurrection will begin,

the restoration of these skeletons
back to life. And birds will
migrate here and animals
emerge from hibernation.
I'll be a transient straight line
surrounded by permanent circles.

The Search Party

I see so many faces,
some close, others in the distance,
a few I know though most are strangers,
trudging through forest,
on a late June afternoon,
scouring tree and pond,
rock ledge and ravine,
for the lost boy.

We're like a phalanx of townspeople,
moving forward while the light still holds,
and spread wide enough to cover all the territory,
not just the trails.
The loudest voices shout the boy's name.
The keenest ears listen for a response.

The light is fading
but not the determination,
as we plunge in and out of thick bracken,
uncaring of any nicks and scratches,
each with a picture in our head
of coming across a child
curled up under an oak tree,
his face shedding tears
in anticipation of what such a find
would do for our faces,
when stripped of everything but our feelings.

There is an ending to our quest
but that's another story.
It's told by the ones who volunteered,
who give no thought to dropping out,
to turning back,
who look near, who look far,
who see so many faces.

Bulbs

Damn.
Sun's going down.
I could be lonely
when it's totally dark.

Just imagine.
The only light
in my life
will be attached to the ceiling,
flicked on
by my finger on the switch.

There'll be no other.
No touch
that isn't of my hands' own making.
No words
that I don't speak.

For all the sun's power,
it can't stay in the sky forever.
Shadows are already
taking up position.
A half-moon
is in the wings.

Daylight isn't much
but at least we humans share.
Darkness lacks community.
Bulbs are solitary.
And they are easily replaced.

Card Table

A card table,
unfulfilled,
does everything but talk
or do the puzzles in the newspaper.

No more games,
needs something else to do,
or it's just a relic
of long-ago Friday nights
of poker, cigarettes and beer.

A sideline,
acting maybe,
King Lear,
all grief, all hardship,
all the time.

She says,
"It has to go."
It's not part of her heart
the way it is for him.

But maybe
she's right.
Why keep
what can only be seen
in retrospect?

A card table,
left out for trash pickup,
winds blow,
fires rage,
thunder shakes,
thunderbolt strikes,
singes its green felt.

'Tis foul.

The Couple In The Photo

In the photograph, he's an ox in human guise.
They say when he split wood,
the valley shuddered.
And she's no frail gamin herself.
That's the pose of a woman
who rejoiced in his hard thundering.

But this is not how they are in life.
They're in the last stages of married-until-death,
feeling shunted aside no doubt,
and barely of this world.

"Yes," he says, "we both were strong
but that was years ago."
She adds, "Everyone from our day is either dead.
Or wishes they were."

They stare at the snapshot
and then at each other's parched, wrinkled faces.
It's the same couple alright.
But time has made prior arrangements.

Forest Floor

Organic horizon,
floss of detritus,
various stages of decomposition
yet each so singular,

bark caressed by fungi,
or trapping algae,
the kingdom of archaea,

a suede of energy,
a sheath of forest skin,
lithe and flexible,
crackling or muted damp,

such subtleties of downward pressure,
brief but intimate,
synchrony of footstep
and the firm ground underneath.

Precocious

First day of school:
a hundred or so variations on dread.
Some are anxious to get
their kiddie greetings over with.
I'm with the group that play dumb.
If there was a way to lock myself
inside my body, I'd do it.
Then I'd flush the key down the toilet.

Loud boys gather together.
Snotty girls do too.
I am in no mood to let
anyone know anything about me.
So I form a clique of one.

I will not divulge the details
of my comic book collection.
Or why I have no father at home.
I value what I do when I am alone.
I've no wish to have it tarnished.

Everybody in class is learning names.
I give up mine reluctantly.
I fear it is a way into me.
I block intrusion
by knowing I'm smarter
than the rest of them.
Even the teacher.

Unfortunately, I'm forced
to sit next to someone.
He looks at me excitedly
like this is the first step
in we two being friends for life.
I tell him that I have
a communicable disease.
He has no idea
what I am talking about.
I take this as an opportunity
to accept the inevitable.

A Connecticut Mill Town

From the shadow of the bridge
I see the mills off in the distance:
rotting benches, rusting machinery,
cavernous rooms
full of lazy light and sated spiders.

It's like a graveyard
where the bodies are lowered
into the ground
but the great brick coffins
remain behind.

The ones who would mourn
are long gone.
The ones who still
earn a living there
are pigeons cooing from the rooftops.

Frank, Legal At Last

He lowered his bones
into his favorite soft squishy armchair,
gathered his papers and weed around him
like the grandchildren he never had.

Then he rolled a spliff so fat and long,
the hand with the pinky ring
on the tiniest of wrinkled fingers
could barely hold onto it.

Then, with a twist of a wrist,
he planted the doobie in between his lips,
lit the far end,
and then inhaled his first ever legal puff.

At age seventy-seven, the law, at last,
had made an honest man of him.

But then someone knocked on the door,
and he hurriedly put out the blunt,
stuffed it under a cushion.

Old habits die hard.
So do the habits that surround those habits.

The Box

Whatever's in this well-wrapped cardboard box
sitting on my front step, I've no idea.
For I didn't order it.
And I'm apprehensive for what it contains.

The name and address on the front
are definitely mine.
But there's no return address,
no way of knowing who it's from.
So I'm concerned.

I stare at the package but I don't have X-ray vision.
I hold it to my ear but it's not a shell.
Then I shake the thing.
The resultant silence appalls me.
I seek answers but I dread them just the same.

I place the parcel on the sideboard,
wash my hands under the tap
just in case another's touch rubbed off on mine.

Then I consider my options.
I could throw it in the fire.
Or smash it to pieces with a sledgehammer.
Or just toss it in the trash.
But I'd still be the owner
for it comes with my name.

My best bet is to hold onto the box
but leave it unopened.
My curiosity won't like it.
But my fear will understand.

Delayed Flight

Another terminal. Another plastic seat.
A screen above my head. Arrivals and departures.

Outside, a clear sky at least.
No wind. No clouds.
Nothing to hinder the day's levitations.

In an hour, I'll be aloft.
The man next to me will doze off.
I'll look at a map of everywhere the airline flies.
A woman will ask, "What would you like to drink?"

I'll look down, with bird's eyes,
at the patchwork.
Farms. Towns. Rivers.
Maybe even a city
where the traffic seems to move.
(Unlike any city I know)

But, until then, I wait.
It's the part of the journey
where there is no taxiing
to the top of the runway,
no takeoff,
no stewardess,
no warm greeting from the captain.

It's plastic seat stage.
It's screen above my head stage.

It's arrivals and departures stage.
Then it's the stage of
the disembodied voice saying,
"Your flight has been delayed."

So, in an hour, I'll be looking forward
to the hour after that.

The Son Curse

I keep staring in the full-length mirror,
naked from the waist up.
I'm flat and pale from throat to navel
except for a slight ridge where the ribs show through.
But no abs, no pecs, nothing approaching tone.

And, in the background,
I can hear my father taking an axe to wood,
blade crunching through oak so fierce
that poor tree doesn't stand a chance.
So what can I fell?
My arms stretch from shoulder
to middle finger without the merest
hint of a contour.
Not even flexing can pop a bean of muscle
out from the frustrating plane.

Later, he'll be half under the car,
digging into that auto's underbelly
with powerful hands and an eye
for how the pieces are supposed to fit.
I'll hang back against the garage door,
staring at his ancient black sneakers,
older than me by all accounts.

Or he'll ask after my homework.
It's already done but,
until he gives it the approval,

it’s merely some numbers,
names and dates dreamed up
by a boy in his early teens.

I’d much rather be
with kids my own age.
It’s easier to amount to something.

Superior Product

An advertising sign blares
against a backdrop of blue sky and scattered clouds,

drawing the attention of both women and men,
now suddenly convinced there is a far

superior washing powder to the one they
have been using. It's in a box, as powerful

as the American military in the Second World War.
A grinning boy, a real boy, shining like God's aura.

A mother with a smile so broad
like she's just accepted

the Congressional Medal of Honor
for duties on the home front.

For just one precious moment,
in an otherwise uneventful day,

the washing comes out clean and bright
and darkens the dreams of our enemies.

A Life In Theory

A life can fit into a plastic bag,
hang with the old men in the park.
It can have a bench to lie down on
and empty eyes with which to see.

A life can take shelter under trees,
scour trash barrels for sustenance.

But then friends and family come for it,
bring it back to where they say it belongs.
A life is often how it imagines itself
when it's not the life it's living.

Interacting With A Famous Guy

You're in the newspaper all the time
and on television twice a week at least,
and you give this impression
of being always out of breath,
as if you're rushed everywhere,
your fame so selfish
there's barely time for bathroom trips.

And look at me:
my mother doesn't recognize me,
the postman delivers my mail to the
house next door,
I haven't one solitary fan
except for the overhead one
that doesn't work anyhow
and my telephone is held in reserve
for telemarketers and wrong numbers.

So how about an autograph?
My life
doesn't have one.

Following The Wake Of Aunt June

Sorry, I can't tell you
how elephants die.

All I know is that
their graveyard
is a secret one,
in the middle of savanna,
or dense jungle.

You're old enough to understand
that death comes to us all
like shadow that keeps spreading
beyond the culpability
of our bodies.

But elephants?
I don't think
that kind of darkness bothers them.
They're not philosophers.
They don't write poetry.

Whether it's the pain in the knee joints
or the deterioration of their teeth,
they're more attuned
to it being their time
and leave the herd appropriately.

Where they go to die remains a mystery.
And now you're asking me

about elephant heaven.
Two mysteries for the price of one -
is that it?

All I know is
that the baby elephant
does not ask its mother
inane questions.

The truth is that
the elephant is the
largest, heaviest land mammal.
And yet its death
is taken lightly.

Mill Town

Along the bank fronted by abandoned mills,
rats drink toxic wastes. It slithers down rat-like.
A solitary mallard skims brown water.
Foul smells, old tires...can a duck have apocalyptic visions?
Through cracks in cement paths,
weeds apologize for sprouting.
Against the mill walls, they cling, they flaunt,
like old-timers begging for jobs.
At river's edge, they glow fluorescent like the fish.

This industry is in its old age, in retirement.
It's an old boot with a rusty hole in the sole.
It's a broken-down woman on the sidewalk,
eyes closed, mouth slightly open,
arthritic knees and veins laying track down her skin.
Management says, if it's broke, don't fix it.
There are other opportunities.
Just don't ask us what they are.

Some kids sneak in a mill through broken windows.
They climb atop the hulks of old machinery,
slam bits of iron against the wall.
Industry's corpse, executive spin...
it will all be theirs someday

The Right Company

My head is limp
from overcrowding
and pallid conversation.
I can't stay in this
smoke-filled,
loud-music-sated room any longer.

So I step outside,
embrace the company
of cool breeze
and surrounding darkness.

And you too
slip away from the crowd,
stand out on the stone veranda,
wine glass in your hand,
eyes plumbing the heights of stars.

I'm flopped on the stairs,
with the noise a mere murmur
and the moon glistening
like a witch's fingernails,
the constellations in full regalia.
And there you are,
the night sky's number one fan.

My "hello" is greeted by
"I didn't know I had company."
I'm not at ease

in rooms full of strangers.
I sometimes think the best company
is the kind you don't know you have.

Field Guide And Crow

As best as I could translate
the crow cawed,
"What's he doing in the woods
with a field guide.
Will you look at that, chickadee.
He's bending down
in the wildflowers,
book held high,
illustrations glossy in the sun.
He's fingering the leaf,
sniffing the flower.
And would you believe it.
He's taken out a pen
and checked off tiger lily."
My wife says
he's just warning
other forest denizens
of our intrusion.
But no, I insist.
He's disturbed at my ignorance.
He's upset that I accumulate
the sighting of
living things like baseball cards.
He's concerned that a crow
is nothing more to me
than a page called 'crow.'

Cabin Fever

He wakes up hung over
though he hasn't been drinking –
unless winter is a hundred proof
because he's already had more
than enough of the cold and snow.

Outside,
a car grinds gears on a road
once flat and smooth as a church pew,
but now slippery and sleeted,
spinning wheels like tops.

Day-old coffee is the first
of many weather reports.
As is the turgid country music
on the radio,
some cowboy pleading sorry
for something any guy would do
if given half the chance

He could really go
for some fried eggs and bacon
but he hasn't been shopping
in a week or two
and who knows if the Chevy will start up
once he's done scraping ice
off all its windows.
He'd sell his soul

just to have a little more
than what he needs to get by.

A shovel leans against the wall of the garage.
It stands guard over his procrastination.
He should go dig himself free.
His routine hasn't been the same
since he resigned from it.
But ever since his wife left and the job fell through
and he fell and broke his collar bone and...
ever since is a time without end.

He watches flakes skid down the windowpane.
A man, he agrees, needs something to live for.
January is not in the running.

The Rip-Raw

Love is created under the threat
of mutual destruction
for even the tender base
is composed of
explosive elements.

What we think is
the vitality of feeling
is really a drop into a swirling pit
of violence and dementia.

Being in love,
we live in a constant petrifying state
of imminence
for love's beholden to
the thunderous fusion
of two living beings.

Reasonable people don't get involved.
Lovers have only themselves to love.

Observing The Nest At Close Hand

Sticks, weeds. a strand of hair, even some string –
I'm face to face with where birds live.
No one home at the moment.
Most likely, this tree trunk lair
is abandoned until next spring.

The most disparate of materials
are so skillfully woven together.
And the placement is the perfect wedge.
It would take a tornado to budge it.
Makes me think of those people
who erect cottages on the shoreline
as if the sea levels will be considerate
in their incessant rising.

There's even some plastic here,
tossed away carelessly by humans,
but adapted well enough by the local birdlife.
No, nothing incriminating here.
The fault continues to lie elsewhere.

Saturday Night In The City

Filament catches flame
in a party girl's eye,
blind angels see nothing but possibilities,
lovelies step from taxis legs first
as a stumbling drunkard
rotates like a color wheel.
From club to sidewalk,
brightness blinks
equal measure of good life and insanity,
lights fueled with enough brilliance
that any face can be adored,
form a network
of blue/red incandescence
as midnight on the clock,
jerks down the beer lever,
ale gushes as free
as a bartender's advice —
mankind should never be saved from this.
Even people with no cachet
can push the button,
screw in the bulbs.
Every shine has purpose
from a wallflower's pallid skin
to a diner's broken sign
to the glitter of the brown canal.
It's not just moths
who dance around the lanterns.

The Next Ten

We sit in the waiting room, ten of us,
same clean, neat hair-cuts, same
gray suits, same faces eager to begin.
And look at the complexions.
You could switch our skin around like
game pieces and not even our
best friends would know the difference.

We don't say anything. We don't have to.
Why ask the one next to me what brought
him to this moment, this chair, his back
straight, arms folded. His story would
just be my story and I already know
my story. So we sit. And we wait.

When the time comes, he will be
very straightforward, we expect. He will
greet us all, shake our hands. We know
his name. He won't bother to learn ours.
He will give us all the same directives,
details different here and there.
He'll explain company policies, dress
code, work responsibilities, end his
spiel with "I'm sure you'll do us proud."
He'll ask, "Any questions?" though there
will be none.

No need even for the interview because
it's like we've been through it beforehand.

Like there's no need to be in this waiting room
with nine other versions of ourselves.
We already have our instructions.
We are what we're instructed to do.

Twilight By The Millrace

I stroll to where the mill race flatters
its abandoned wooden wheel
with nudges, lapping, hints of past glories.
The path is mostly muddy puddles from a midday rain
that see no sense in joining up with other waters,
merely fill the holes they're given,
await the inevitable burn-off as song sparrows
drink this bounty while they can.
The mill's facade changes with the moment
like time-lapse photography
from a documentary on the dying of an industry.
But it's a peaceful place for all that.
Its wooden frame is a haven for swallows.
Its machinery transforms gray into brown.
I love to sit on a plank and sense,
for once, nature as usurper, as pioneer.
And it's reclaiming as gently as the deer
that nibbles on a tuft of grass close by me.
Her head is bowed but one ear's always cocked,
scans the surrounds for alien sound.
Please, wild creature,
accept my breath as an apology.

An Occupied House

An army of the dead occupy these barracks.
One man watches snow shift the world
and yet, preserve it like a dream.
An aftershock, the heirlooms on the mantle rattle and fall.
Now all of them asleep, pieces everywhere, a silent weight,
a farcical resemblance to time and space,
as I wipe my glasses, certain this house talks
like a parrot that stares at the great one for a sign,
as now, at the top of the winding stairs, I am
praying the family sleep through another night.
crying, how is this done, when the frozen
bodies in earth are jostled, cracked,
moving in, their words warm as coals in my ears.

Even if it's only this floating and clinging ether,
it's a truth that leaves me trembling like fumbled prayer.
I can do people no better justice than love them.
But look – my hand glows white on a moon-slicked railing,
my solitude is softened by tender night,
clock on the wall tick-tocks timelessly.
dim photographs of ancestors line the walls,
the dog keeps a wary eye on the one man he loves.
He can taste the flesh of the black air
is drunk with all the scattered pieces surrounding him.

Even in stillness, the house needs to thump,
the colors go slowly white. How many gone before
have come again? Is that a laugh or the boiler of darkness?
The bookshelves are flesh gray. The countertops are frames.

The house is painted with grinning faces.
No use sleeping. My first ever dog will claw me awake.
I can sit for a while with love's flickering darkness,
hear the house-heave of sleepers, and go jittery,
look out through window glass buffeted by rapping knuckles,
see footsteps circling the snow Are those the tracks of a dream world?
Footprints are unassailable when nothing living makes them.

I see the face of some brother in jail betrayed,
bright, ubiquitous malice,
that in later years became a monster,
a punch-drunk threat – and now he pleads
to the winter-shadowed house where I live on.
Were we not inseparable from the start?

Is it up to me to keep him alive,
to fill the house with the best of him,
cut his malicious heart out? I believe I can do this.
Parents do not squander the opportunity.
They glow where cracks fan drafts.
An older sister is that walker in the snow.
An old friend is doing all the whistling.
Night after night, they make their stand.
Door after door leads to them.

People crave flesh like boys gather toys.
The clock is in denial.
A dog is locked out on gleaming icy steps.
Hope is stamped on the brows of the young.
A good chance, so they said. Impassive is my response.
Overhead, giddy stars do cartwheels.
Pipes clank and gargle like an ogre's stomach.
Light plays tricks with my eyes and my head likewise.

I plead. I accuse. The moon is far off and dim,
rising with an idiot's blank yellow face,
shaped by the years when it was a lover's chunk of rock.

Come morning, I hustle downstairs to halt the jackhammers.
And every day I wipe my glasses but still they tear up the street.
Digging into shadows, and the shrieks of old women.
in sub-zero temperatures, as now, morning fire finds an opening,
spreads freely through dark houses. Those enigmatic fissures
eat their young, who could make it given a chance, just
as there is only truth and law. I have learned that law.
I have lived my life tethered to it.

To believe is to extol dust,
to hear breathing in the house of the dead,
to go forward without question or answer,
to allow those who are gone to continue in my head.
Even in an empty house, I can come to know them.
On the magic stairs. In the fairyland beds.
There is no ascending alone to the second floor.
I take a knife blade to the raw facts
when they try to take over my living quarters.
Where I live, the wind howls within reason.
There is no fear I can name that is not a loss to myself.

These Prairie Dogs

The prairie dogs are workaholics.
They have built a city in the soil.
You can feel their bodies warming
together deep inside the earth.
And their voices, no past, no future,
chirp, with what is happening now.

Not so us, bouncing by
in our four-wheel drive
on a long, long highway.
Everything's a coming attraction
or a place you can't get back to.

We get nothing done because there's
these years and years behind us
of it never having been done
and years and years ahead of us
of it never will be done.

But these rodents are yoked
to fragments of time,
as short as they're demanding.
What choice do they have
but to live in them?

Looking Through The Family Album

I speak a different language,
all in glossy color,
all who are old beware -
and to think,
these are dead people,
right in my face -
but you're a dancer - I'm jealous -
crazy shoes,
dear ancient photograph,
every moment just
engaging me in some way -
I'm supposed to be a gust of fresh air
with all these years of me,
but you're the one who's
flashing smiles like neon -
you can steal the heat
from my body
as I thumb through this album -
yes, there's a resemblance,
I would still be you -
I'd kiss you
on the cheek
if not for the years between,
and this boy -
we could play games -
and woman
if you were here,
there's be guys lined up
at the front door –

it's like looking inside of me –
life constantly mutates
maybe once a generation,
this is more fun than intelligence,
the past attacking my flanks,
an only fashioned fight
in which the winner gets to be
the survivor –
okay. I get it –
this dates to the turn of the twentieth century -
it's as if I have always been here,
time is a reward
for making sure
my ancestors are not me.

The Cowboy Trucker

He imagines
the Stetson hat,
the chaps and spurs.

And the horse
beneath him of course.

But it's an eighteen-wheeler
he lowers himself down from,
and he's dressed in jeans
and greasy t-shirt.

This is not a watering-hole,
just a diner.
And he saw no tumbleweeds
getting here,
merely mile after mile
of flat mid-west.

He plops down
on a counter stool,
and does say
"Howdy" instead of "Hi."

He orders cold beer
and a steak.
And later,
a tank-full for his herd.

Reunions

I hate reunions.
There's some who really made it.
Others who failed.
The rest of us converge in the middle.

It's painful.
Mediocrities have nothing to say to each other.
If I was a success,
I could brag about it.

Or a bum on the streets,
I could honestly moan.
But we're all thinking,
had we tried harder,

then we'd be the ones
raking in the dough.
Or we really did try hard
and yet look where we are.

Or maybe if we hadn't tried at all,
we'd be so much happier.
We don't express anything of that of course.
It's more like,

"You're putting on a little weight"
and "A few gray hairs there, buddy boy."

I despise reunions.
I'm heavier, going gray

And all I have to show for it
is other people like me.

Progress Of A Kind

In northern New Hampshire,
beyond the White Mountains,
in crusty November air,
I saw fences crumbling,
fields overgrown with weed
and tall shapeless grass,
dilapidated farmhouses
and sagging-roofed barns
turning to the seed of wood
and metal and glass.

The forest was reclaiming
this miscarried farm,
maples, firs, alders,
evicting the orchards, the grain crops,
the lingering stench of cow patties.
Wildflowers sprouted
in the remnants of gardens.
Vines wrapped around
an abandoned tractor.

The truth is that
sometimes man gets it wrong.
Then nature steps in
and does it right.

ACKNOWLEDGEMENTS

Poem	Publication
A Connecticut Mill Town	Third Wednesday
A Life In Theory	Muddy River Poetry Review
A Suburban News Update	City Brink
An Intuit Boy	Glitterati
An Occupied House	Ginosko Literary Review
Bittersweet	Abbey
Bulbs	In Parentheses
Cabin Fever	Treehouse
Card Table	Open: Journal Of Arts And Letters
Dead Man?	Avant Appalachia
Dear Friend	Metonym
Delayed Flight	Spire Light
Explaining My Heart To You	Winamop
Field Guide And Crow	Lamplit Underground
Following The Wake Of Aunt June	In Parentheses
For Worse	Pure Slush
Forest Floor	Caesura
Frank, Legal At Last	Floyd County Moonshine
If You Wish To Know My Current Location	Viridian Door
In A World That Only Involves Ducks	Wilderness House
In Ghoul World	Pomona Valley Review
Indian Summer	Wilderness House
Interacting With A Famous Guy	Corvus Review
Looking Through The Family Album	Ginosko Literary Review
Mill Town	Haight-Ashbury Literary Journal

My Collection	Prairie Wolf Review
Observing The Nest At Close Hand	Pegasus
Precocious	Stoneboat
Progress Of A Kind	Cantos
Reunions	Homestead Review
Saturday Night In The City	Beechwood Review
Suburbia, On Any Given Day	Euphony Journal
Superior Product	Poetry Breakfast
The Beauty Begins Here	Mycellum
The Box	Haight-Ashbury Literary Journal
The Car Alarm	Beliveau Review
The Couple In The Photo	Prairie Wolf Review
The Cowboy Trucker	Floyd County Moonshine
The Family Wanderer	Abbey
The Guy At The Open Mike	Poetry Superhighway
The Lessons In Arguing	Write Place At The Write Time
The Next Ten	Confluence
The Poem Of The Hunters	Home Planet News
The Right Company	Creosote
The Rip-Raw	Origami
The Search Party	Canyon Voices
The Son Curse	Trajectory
The Sonnet Of The Forest	The Orchards
These Prairie Dogs	Globe Review
To A Cop Found Hanging	Hidden Chapter
To The Fox	Page And Spine
Tropical Escape	Avalon
Twilight By The Millrace	Voices De La Luna
Walking In The Winter Forest	River And South

www.ingramcontent.com/pod-product-compliance
Ingram Content Group UK Ltd.
Pitfield, Milton Keynes, MK11 3LW, UK
UKHW041315190726
13845UKWH00025B/287

9 789363 545809